no rhyme. no reason

paulanthonywilson

contents:

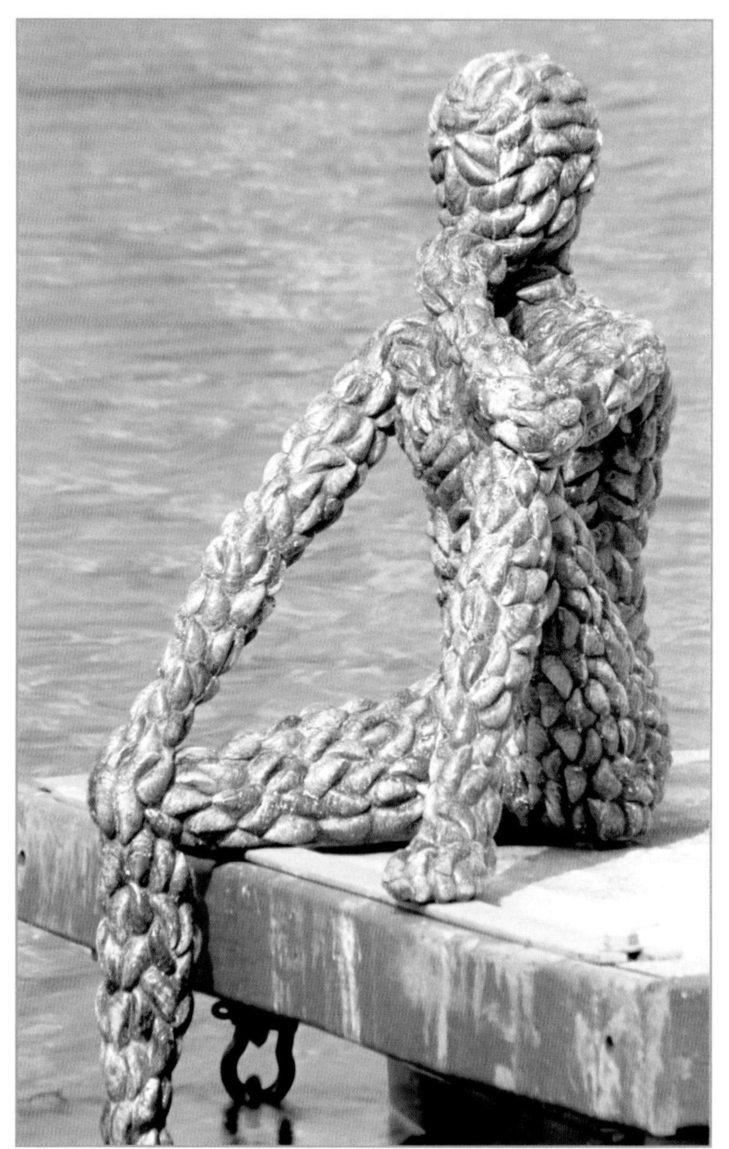

Introduction:

Born in Hull on the 23rd September 1956.
Discovered a passion for photography 1986.
Turned professional 1992.

No rhyme, no reason is a collection of images covering a wide subject range.

The chapter 'Close to home' covers well known local scenes from an entirely different perspective, such as 'under Whitby's east pier' the 'swing bridge' and 'fireworks over St. Mary's' 'Endeavour arriving in 1997' also became a momentus event when entering the harbour again after over 250 years.

'North to south, coast to coast' looks at a selection of images taken 'here and there', with hopefully,the emphasis on humour! 'Blackpool tandoori' highlights our changing culture, influenced by our integration with other nationalities, even our traditional seaside holiday, where once there was fish & chips, candyfloss, donuts and ice cream, there are now 'promenade' indian takeaways. Scarborough has a tradition on Shrove Tuesday where the south foreshore is closed off, the local children then receive a half day holiday from school to go skipping, the Mayor Eileen Bosomworth is seen here taking part.

'East side locals' puts faces to names of the people who have worked tirelessly to protect the unique atmosphere of Whitby.
Artist John Freeman, who with his watercolour paintings has enhanced Whitby's history with pictures such as 'The Pull' and the 'Return of the Endeavour'.
Dorothy Clegg or as she is known locally 'Councillor Clegg' dedicates almost all of her time, on various committees and as a councillor on the Scarborough borough council fighting for Whitby's corner.

Dick Hoyle is another well known figure, not just for his eccentric appearance, but for his commitment to several local causes and his stalwart defence of Whitby, he and his wife Pam, run their shop 'Bobbins' which is the old chapel on Church street.
All of the people in this section have contributed something to this community and generations to come will put faces to the names, that will surely crop up many times, like Mike Wray the busker who not only gives an ambience to the streets with his sea shanties but plays the harp, leads ghost walks and his Punch & Judy is second to none.
Shop owners that keep alive traditional trades, such as William and his family at the 'Black Market' Sandgate, still make by hand, Whitby jet jewellery, Justin of 'Justin's Fudge' church street supplies visiting goths with his famous chocolate 'coffins', Allan at curios corner who specializes in collectable toys and Steve & Wendy Wood who stock just about every sweet you can think of in their 'old world' sweet shop on sandgate.
Dave Noble used to sit on church street outside of his cottage, tourists would say hello to him because they thought he was passing the time of day, he wasn't, he was cursing at them.

Most people visiting Whitby would see me taking 'Victorian Style Portraits' in the 'Victorian Image' on Sandgate, no rhyme. no reason is to showcase my previously unseen work.
Frank Meadow Sutcliffe was a portrait photographer earning 'a crust' in Whitby during the Victorian period, but it was not his studio images that gave him his worldwide acclaim, it was the documentary style pictures of 'life' in Whitby at that time.
In my own way I am trying to continue his work and hope that one day my images will give an insight to the past, just as his do today.
Unlike Frank Meadow my pictures are not limited to Whitby but stretch up and down the country, with images in France and North Africa also included.

close to home

East Pier Whitby

road to Beck Hole

Saltburn Beach

Whitby Regatta

Whitby Abbey

Whitby Abbey

Whitby Swing Bridge

Whitby

Endeavour arrives in Whitby 1997

north to south,coast to coast

Glasgow

Yorkshire Sculpture Park

Blackpool Tandoori

Blackpool Tramlines

View from the Tate

Tate Modern

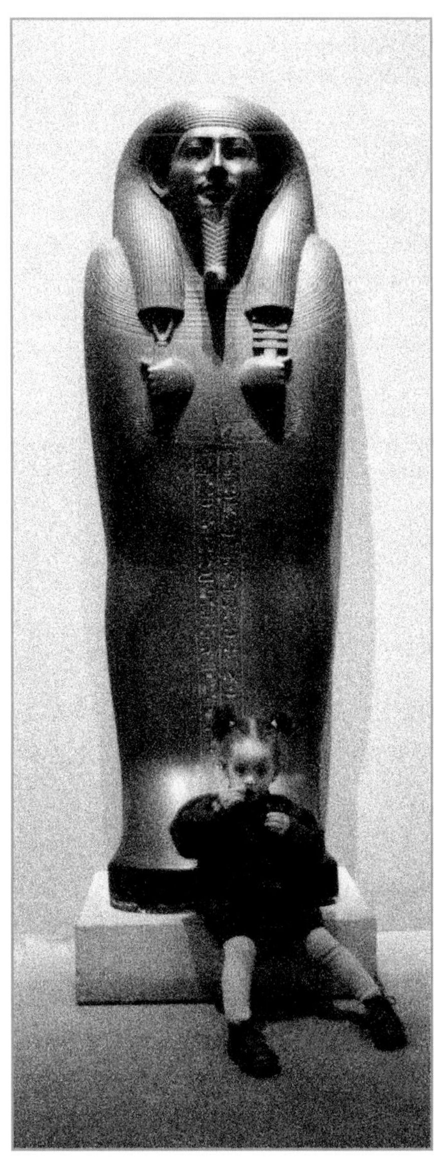

me and my mummy

Harrods

all my own work

'breakfast' Seamer Horse Fair

'trotting' Seamer Horse Fair

'gypsy strongman' Leo Wilson

fairground worker

fundraising in Whitby

the Pierrottas at Filey

skipping day

Market Place, Whitby

Captain Cook street entertainer

gypsy kids

the kids of today...

whale watching

spring fashion

Annie

MUSTON
SCARECROW
FESTIVAL
& COMPETITION
24TH JULY - 1ST AUGUST

MOLES
ARE
REVOLTING

pro fox hunt demo

Saltburn Pier

east side locals

artist John Freeman

Dorothy Clegg

Allan Barsby, ‘curios corner’ Whitby

William Moralee, 'black market' jet shop

Justin 'Justin's Fudge'

Steve Wood Sandgate 'sweety' shop

Mike Wray 'the busker'

Dick Hoyle

Dave Noble

the french connection

pumpkins, Montmartre

Moulin Rouge

wine vats, Cognac

Fouras

the Louvre

classic car, La Rochelle

La Rochelle

the French house

La Rochelle

Champs Elysees

north africa

Citroen, Sousse, Tunisia

Morocco

Ribat, cat

El Djem amphitheatre

Chott El Jerid, salt flats

Tunisian gossip

shopping

Morocco

local butchers shop

waterseller, Marrakesh

Djemaa El Fna, Marrakesh

animals

Knowlsley Safari Park

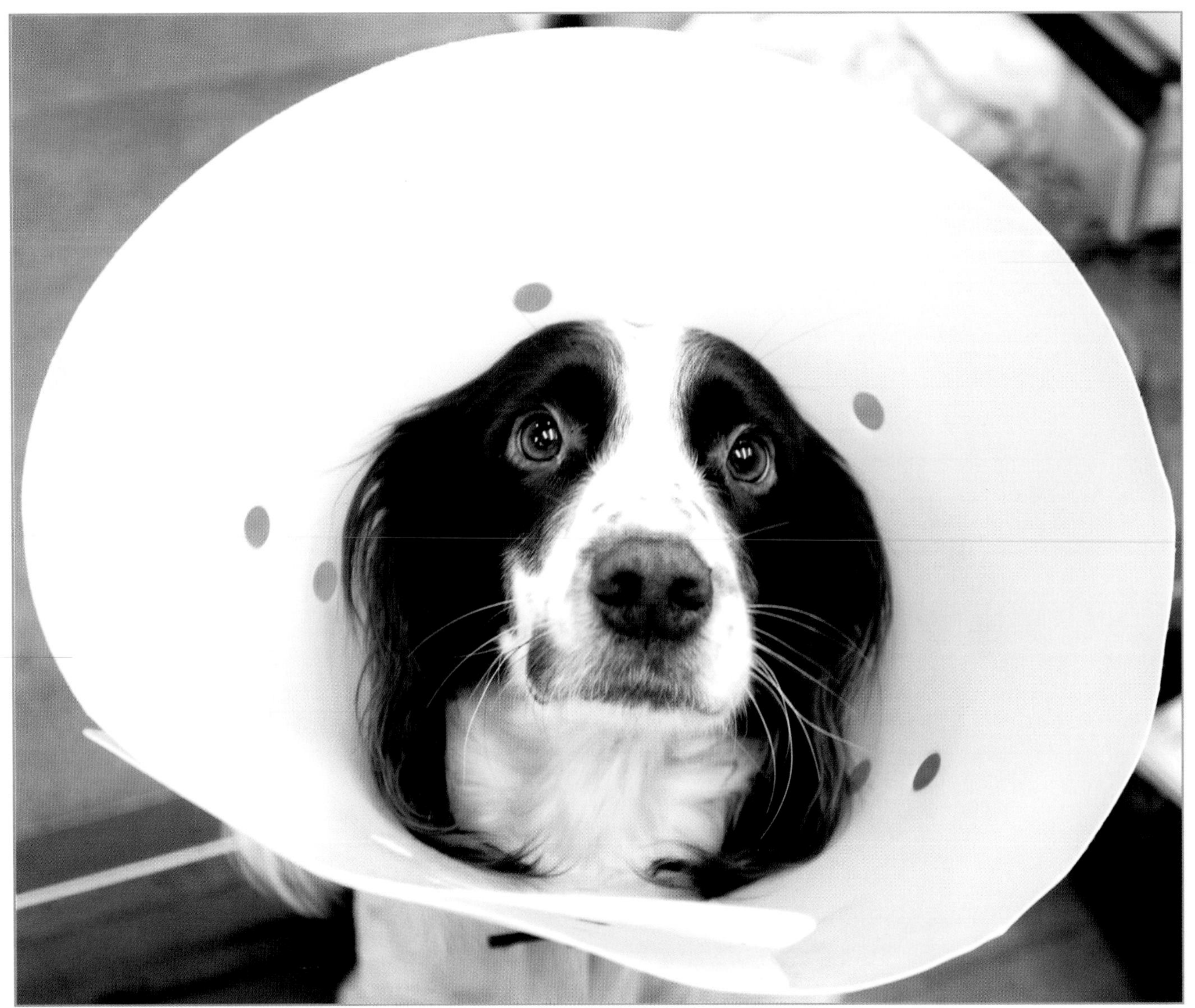

Spot the dog

Spanish dog

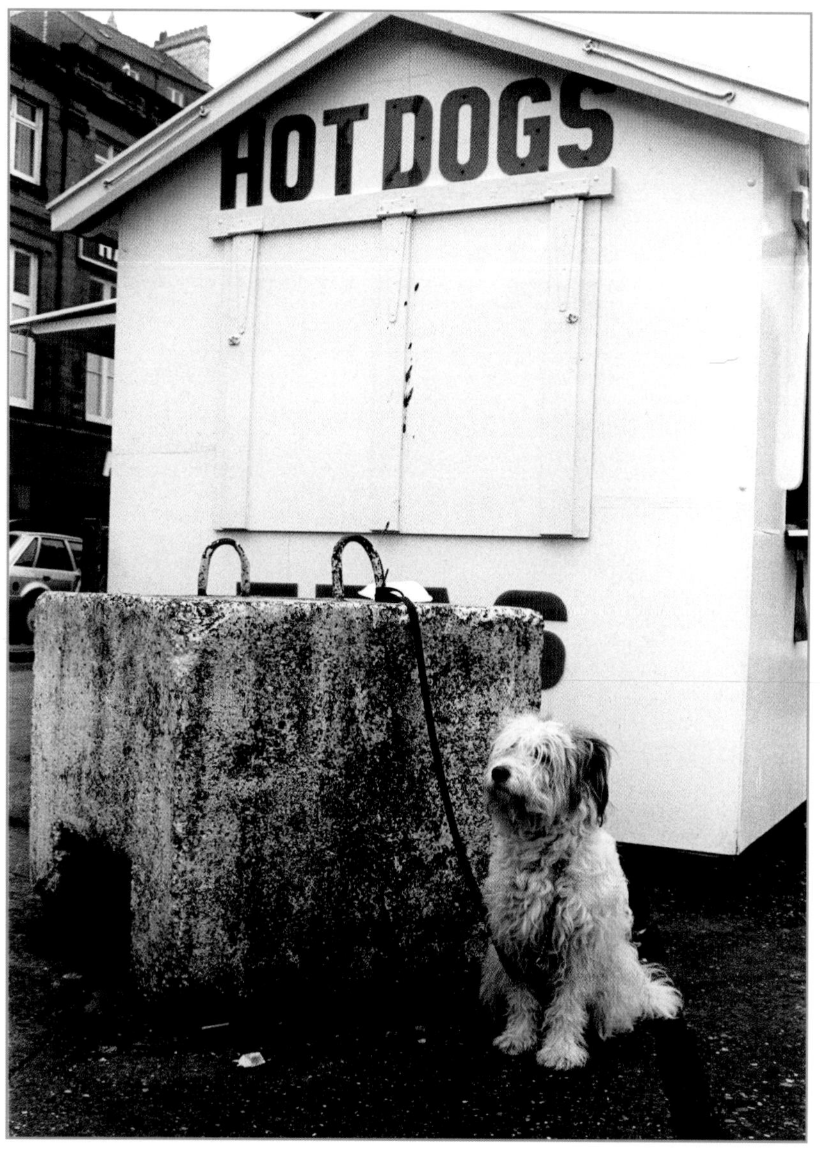

Whitby 'fresh' hot dog stall

Andalucian dog

otter

highland cow

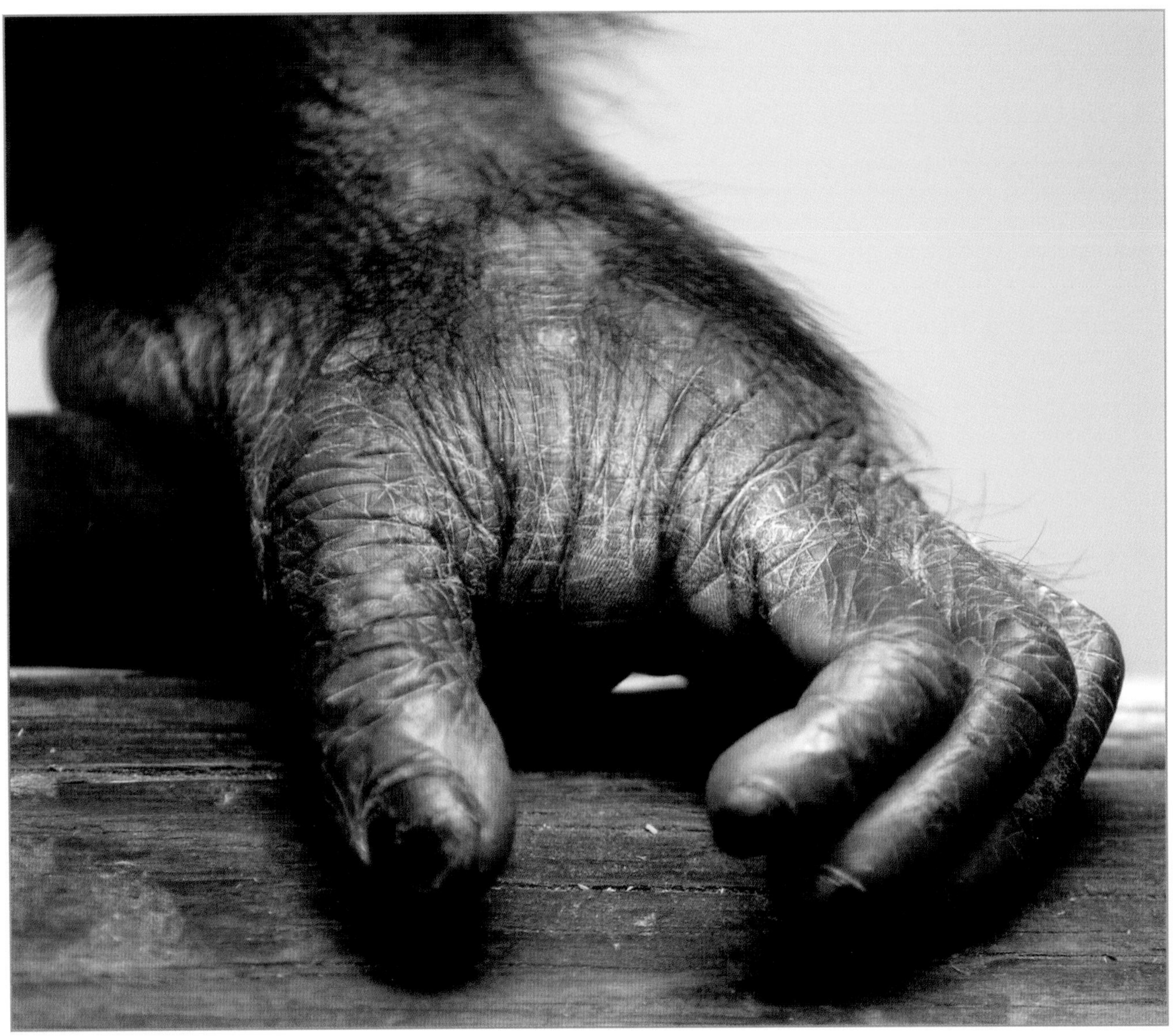

chimp's hand

meerkat sentry guards

meerkats playfighting

meerkat relaxing

pig racing

ferret racing

sheep racing

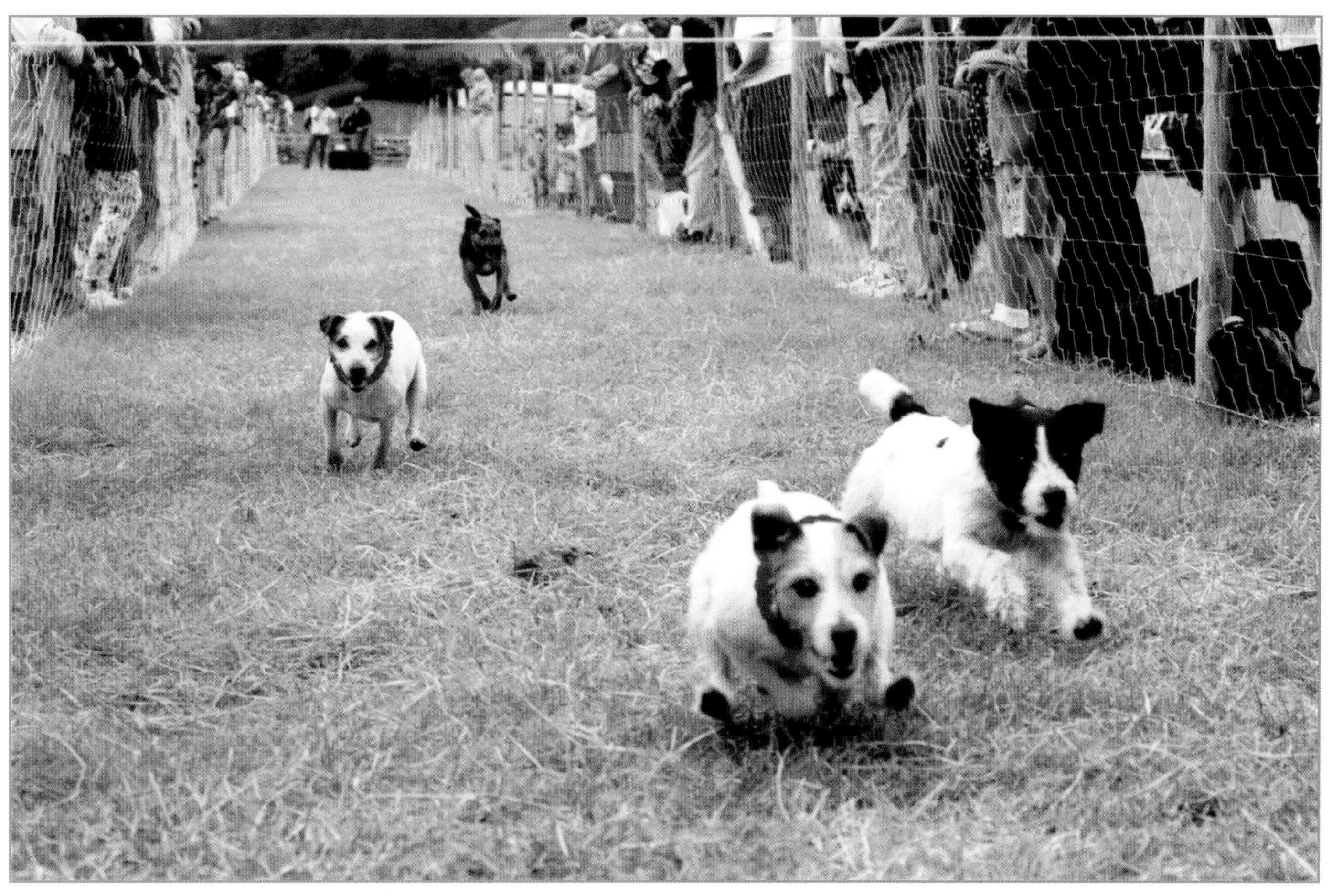

terrier racing

on the wall

all points...

conkers

braking wave

night snow dune

snow road

fern

cricket ball

Durness

'posts' Loch Linnie

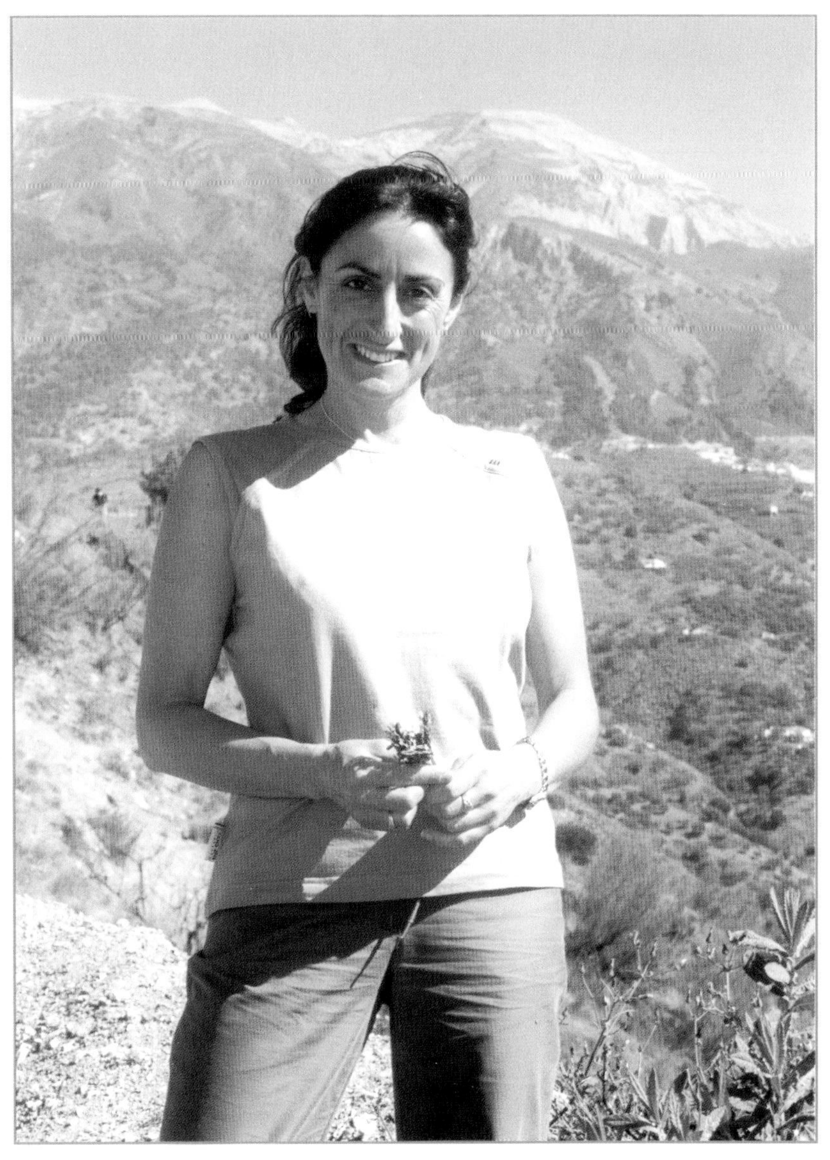

Lynne, the love of my life

photograph: Lynne Valentine

published by 'paulanthonywilson'

Paul Anthony Wilson
17 Cromwell Road
Scarborough
YO11 2DR
e-mail: victorianimage99@aol.com

designed by paul anthony wilson & lynne valentine
printed by Falcon Press (Stockton-on-Tees) Ltd.

ISBN 0-9550074-0-2